DRAW SCOOBY-DOO!

Monsters, Robots, Aliens, and MORE!

by Steve Korté

illustrated by Scott Jeralds

CAPSTONE PRESS
a capstone imprint

TABLE OF CONTENTS

Let's Draw with Scooby-Doo!................... 4

What You'll Need............................ 5

Scooby-Doo................................ 8

Shaggy 10

Daphne 12

Fred.................................... 14

Velma................................... 16

The Mystery Machine 18

Scrappy-Doo.............................. 20

Scooby-Dum............................. 22

Yabba-Doo 24

Scooby-Dee............................. 26

Monster Truck Mystery Machine 28

On the Case!............................ 30

The Beast of Bottomless Lake 36

Creepy Heap from the Deep................38

Creature from the Chem Lab 40

Greek Minotaur......................... 42

Gator Ghoul............................ 44

Jaguaro................................ 46

Demon Shark........................... 48

Abominable Snowman 50

Octopus Monster....................... 52

MYSTERY INC. AND FRIENDS

CREEPY CREATURES

Mantis..................................... 54

Unmasking the Gator Ghoul................... 56

The Green Ghosts 62

10,000 Volt Ghost 64

Phantom 66

Black Knight 68

Ghost Clown................................ 70

Redbeard's Ghost........................... 72

The Creeper................................ 74

Miner Forty Niner 76

Ghost of Captain Cutler 78

Ghost of Mr. Hyde 80

Escaping the Ghost Clown.................... 82

Charlie the Funland Robot 88

Snow Beast 90

Spooky Space Kook 92

Future Monster 94

Evil Alien 96

Rawhide Red 98

Mars Robot.................................100

Monster Mouse 102

Nuclear Alien 104

Body-Snatcher Alien 106

Escaping Charlie the Funland Robot 108

GHOSTS AND GHOULS

ROBOTS AND ALIENS

LET'S DRAW WITH SCOOBY-DOO!

ZOOM!

A brightly colored van charges down the road on a moonlit night. A cool and confident teenager named Fred Jones is behind the wheel. Sitting next to him are his fearless friends Velma Dinkley and Daphne Blake. Behind them, in the back of the van, is a nervous dude named Shaggy Rogers and an even more nervous Great Dane named Scooby-Doo.

The colorful van is called the Mystery Machine. The five passengers are known as Mystery Incorporated—a talented team that solves spooky mysteries around the globe.

When ghosts are gathering, monsters are menacing, and robots are rampaging . . . don't panic! Mystery Inc. is on the way to save the day!

Over the years, Scooby and the gang have solved mysteries and captured a whole host of terrifying ghosts and monsters. Now it's time for you to draw them!

WHAT YOU'LL NEED

You are about to draw the world's most famous mystery-solving team and their most fearsome foes! But you'll need some basic tools to draw them. Gather the following supplies before starting your awesome art.

paper

You can get special drawing paper from art supply and hobby stores. But any type of blank, unlined paper will work fine.

pencils

Drawings should always be done in pencil first. Even the pros use them. If you make a mistake, it'll be easy to erase and redo it. Keep plenty of these essential drawing tools on hand.

pencil sharpener

To make clean lines, you need to keep your pencils sharp. Get a good pencil sharpener. You'll use it a lot.

erasers

As you draw, you're sure to make mistakes. Erasers give artists the power to turn back time and undo those mistakes. Get some high-quality rubber or kneaded erasers. They'll last a lot longer than pencil erasers.

black marker pens

When your drawing is ready, trace over the final lines with a black marker pen. The black lines will help make your characters stand out on the page.

colored pencils and markers

Ready to finish your masterpiece? Bring your characters to life and give them some color with colored pencils or markers.

MYSTERY INC. AND FRIENDS

Scooby-Doo

Scooby-Doo is the only canine member of Mystery Inc. Named Scoobert at birth, this cowardly Great Dane loves to scarf down Scooby Snacks, but he's not a big fan of cornering creepy creatures. When faced with a mysterious monster or gruesome ghoul, Scooby will cry, "Ruh-roh!" and look for a quick exit.

1

dRawing idea
Draw a tasty triple-decker sandwich next to Scooby.

2

3

4

5

Shaggy

1

Norville "Shaggy" Rogers is Scooby-Doo's very best friend. The two are rarely apart and often leap into each other's arms when something scares them. Shaggy also tends to goof off, and he is almost always hungry. When he's not tracking down monsters, Shaggy is usually on the hunt for a tasty snack, such as a cheese pizza with pickles.

2

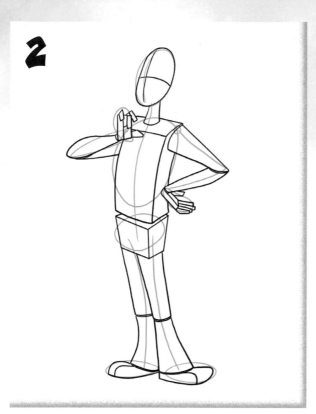

3

4

5

Daphne

1

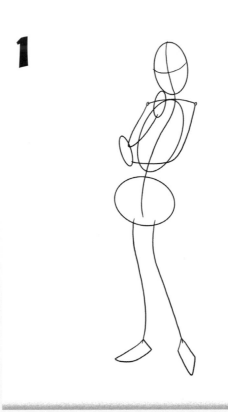

Daphne Blake's skills as an investigator stem from her background as a journalist. While nothing makes her happier than solving a good mystery, she also has a knack for getting into trouble. It's no wonder her nickname is Danger-Prone Daphne! While battling ghosts, ghouls, and other creepy creatures, it's not uncommon to hear her cry, "Jeepers!"

2

3

4

5

Fred

Fred Jones, Jr. is the unofficial leader of the Mystery Inc. gang. He is athletic, brave, and very well dressed—pretty much the opposite of Shaggy. Fred usually drives the Mystery Machine, and he is the most likely member of the team to declare, "Hey gang! It looks like we have a mystery to solve!"

1

dRawing idea

The next time you draw Fred, show him next to the Mystery Machine.

2

3

4

5

Velma

Velma Dinkley is the youngest and the smartest member of Mystery Inc. When there are creatures to catch or monsters to unmask, Velma uses her brilliant brain to follow the clues and save the day. Just about the only thing that can stop her is if she loses her glasses, causing her to say, "Jinkies! I can't see a thing without my glasses!"

1

dRawing idea
The next time you draw Velma, show her pulling a sheet off someone dressed as a ghost.

2

3

4

5

The Mystery Machine

1

How does the Mystery Inc. gang travel from one mystery to another? In their ultra-groovy Mystery Machine, of course! This super-cool van serves as the team's mobile headquarters and comes with a high-tech computer, a three-person scooter, and several boxes of Scooby Snacks for Shaggy and Scooby.

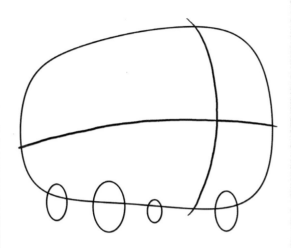

2

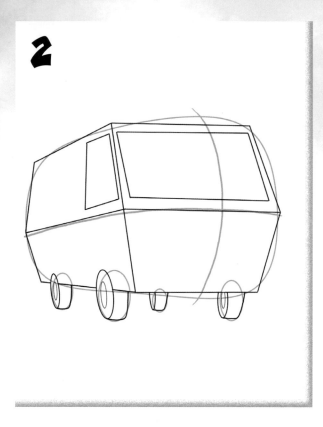

3

4

5

Scrappy-Doo

He's only five years old, but the pint-sized Scrappy-Doo has a lot of "puppy power!" He's Scooby-Doo's nephew, and—unlike his uncle—is one courageous canine. In fact, Scrappy sometimes leaps into action before he thinks, which can cause trouble.

1

dRawing idea

Draw Scooby-Doo next to Scrappy-Doo. Scooby is four times bigger than Scrappy!

2

3

4

5

Scooby-Dum

Scooby-Dum is Scooby-Doo's not-so-smart cousin. He lives in the Hokefenokee Swamp with restaurant owners, Ma and Pa Skillet. Although he often hinders Scooby and the gang more than he helps them, Scooby-Dum's kind and earnest nature is hard to resist.

1

dRawing idea

Add a spooky swamp background behind Scooby-Dum.

2

3

4

5

Yabba-Doo

Way out West, Scooby-Doo has a crime-fighting canine brother named Yabba-Doo. Yabba is owned by Deputy Dusty in Tumbleweed County. Unlike Scooby, Yabba is confident and courageous. But he does share his brother's love of food, especially big bowls of Chili Snacks. His favorite phrase is "Yippity-Yabbity-Doo!"

1

dRawing idea
Add a big bowl of chili next to Yabba-Doo.

2

3

4

5

Scooby-Dee

Scooby-Dee is Scooby-Doo's cousin. She is also a famous movie star. By batting her eyes and wagging her tail, she can get other canines—and quite a few people—to do whatever she wants. Her fans from all around the world just love it when she says, "Fiddle dee dee!"

1

dRawing idea

Show Scooby-Dee on a movie set. Add a movie camera and a director.

2

3

4

5

Monster Truck Mystery Machine

When Shaggy wins a trip to a tropical island, he brings the Mystery Inc. team with him. It turns out that the island is really the setting for a new zombie movie, and the gang has been tricked into making an appearance in the film. Even more remarkable is a deluxe Monster Truck version of the Mystery Machine driven by Fred's stunt double!

1

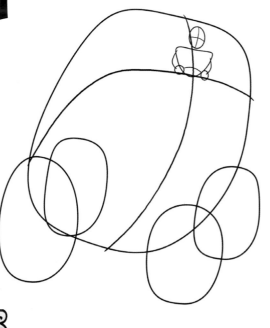

drawing idea
Add a hairy zombie monster standing on top of the Monster Truck Mystery Machine.

2

3

4

5

On the Case!

It's a dark, gloomy night in a very creepy forest. The moon is barely shining, and the Mystery Machine rolls slowly down a shadowy road in the forest. Shaggy and Scooby shiver as they peer out the window.

"Like, do you guys see those glowing eyes in the forest?" Shaggy asks.

Fred hits the brakes on the van and turns to his teammates. "Let's go, gang," he says. "We've got a mystery to solve!"

1

4

5

CREEPY CREATURES

The Beast of Bottomless Lake

1

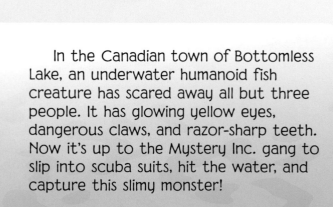

In the Canadian town of Bottomless Lake, an underwater humanoid fish creature has scared away all but three people. It has glowing yellow eyes, dangerous claws, and razor-sharp teeth. Now it's up to the Mystery Inc. gang to slip into scuba suits, hit the water, and capture this slimy monster!

Creepy Heap from the Deep

This freaky-looking monster is guaranteed to spoil any beach party! It has one giant eye, green seaweed atop its head, and dangerously sharp, crablike claws. "Watch out for those claws, gang!" calls out Fred as the Mystery Inc. gang gets ready to battle the Creepy Heap from the Deep.

1

dRawing idea

After you draw this creepy creature, add a frightened Scooby-Doo to your picture.

2

3

4

5

Creature from the Chem Lab

1

A claw-handed monster is scaring the students at Hillside High. Cheerleaders run from the gym screaming in fear when the creature arrives. It's up to Mystery Inc. to find out if the monster was created in the school's chemistry lab. And it's up to you to draw this beast.

2

3

4

5

Greek Minotaur

In old tales of Greek mythology, the Minotaur was a fierce monster with the head of a bull and the body of a man. But Minotaurs don't really exist, right? "Zoinks!" yells Shaggy when he and Scooby meet a raging beast on a Greek island.

1

dRawing idea

Add a scared Shaggy to your drawing of the Minotaur. Maybe show Shaggy dropping his bag of snacks when he sees the monster.

Gator Ghoul

A mysterious alligator creature known as the Gator Ghoul is haunting the Hokefenokee Swamp and scaring away customers at Ma and Pa Skillet's restaurant. Can Scooby-Doo and his cousin Scooby-Dum cook up a way to save the business?

1

dRawing idea

Show Scooby-Doo and his cousin Scooby-Dum chasing the Gator Ghoul.

44

2

3

4

5

Jaguaro

Deep within a Brazilian jungle lurks a massive beast with the body of a brown gorilla and the head of a black saber-tooth tiger. It's the ferocious monster known as the Jaguaro. When the Mystery Inc. gang shows up in that same jungle, Scooby and Shaggy just might end up as snacks for this creepy creature!

1

dRawing idea

Add a jungle background to your drawing. You can include lots of trees and maybe some colorful tropical birds, such as parrots.

2

3

4

5

Demon Shark

1

Maybe it wasn't the smartest thing Scooby-Doo ever did when he decided to eat an egg, cheese, and hot dog sandwich while out water-skiing. That's just the kind of thing that might attract a hungry half-man and half-fish creature known as the Demon Shark!

dRawing idea

The next time you draw the Demon Shark, show him leaping out of the ocean's waves.

48

2

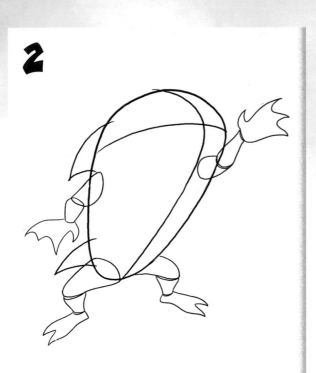

3

4

5

Abominable Snowman

The Abominable Snowman is a giant creature that lives high atop a snow-capped mountain. He is covered from head to toe in white fur, and he has a fierce temper. When Scooby makes the mistake of skiing too close to this dangerous monster, it's up to the rest of the gang to rescue him.

1

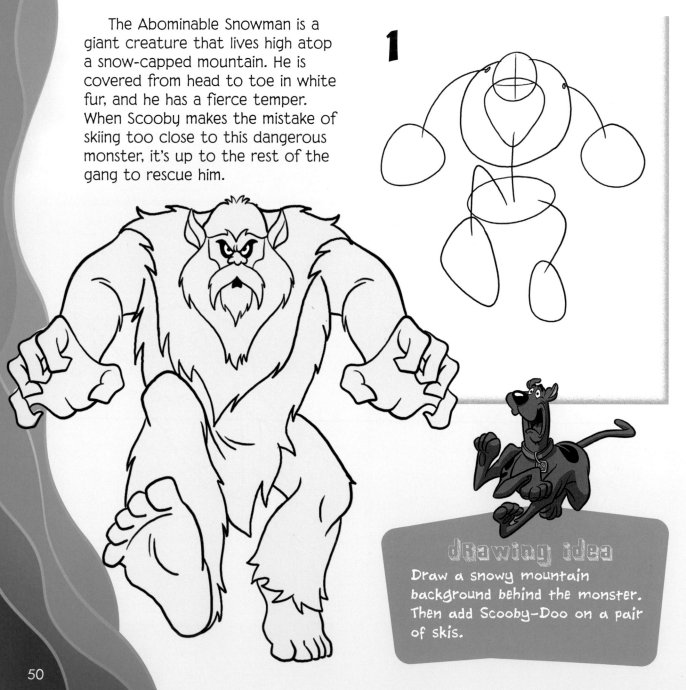

dRawing idea

Draw a snowy mountain background behind the monster. Then add Scooby-Doo on a pair of skis.

2

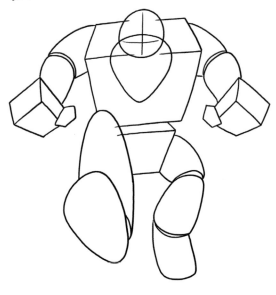

 3

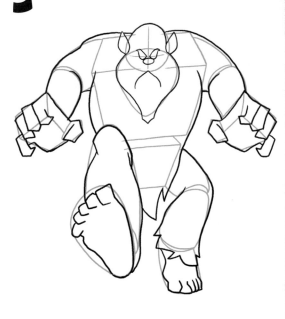

4

 5

Octopus Monster

What has wiggling tentacles, a mouth full of sharp teeth, and a dangerous appetite? It's the Octopus Monster! This slimy creature is guarding a sunken pirate ship filled with treasures—and it will gobble up anyone who gets too close!

1

2

3

4

5

Mantis

1

"Jeepers!' says Daphne while visiting Vulture's Claw Botanical Garden. She has just encountered a terrifying, seven-foot-tall bug known as Mantis. Where did this giant praying mantis come from? Was it the result of an experiment gone wrong? And how will Daphne and the gang escape from it?

2

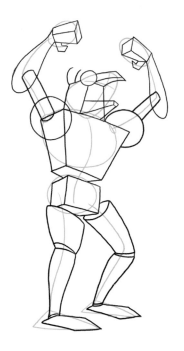

3

4

5

Unmasking the Gator Ghoul

Ruh-roh! The Mystery Inc. gang has cornered the Gator Ghoul in the Hokefenokee Swamp. The monster hisses and flashes its dangerously sharp teeth. "Hang on, gang!" says Fred as he bravely grabs the Gator Ghoul's head and removes its mask. The monster is really an angry restaurant employee named Alice Dovely. Mystery Inc. has saved the day!

1

2

3

4

5

GHOSTS AND GHOULS

The Green Ghosts

Scooby-Doo is going to inherit a large fortune, but there's a catch. In order to collect the money, he and the rest of the Mystery Inc. gang must spend one night in a sinister mansion. Can the team survive a frightful night in a house that is haunted by two green ghosts?

1

dRawing idea

Choose your two favorite members of Mystery Inc. and add them to your drawing of one of the Green Ghosts.

2

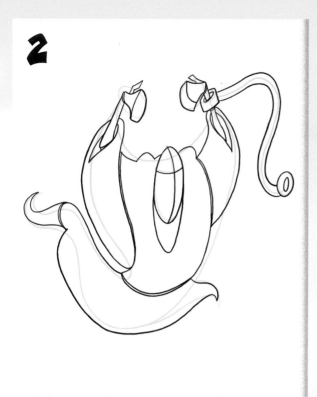

3

4

5

10,000 Volt Ghost

"Jinkies!" yells a frightened Velma when she encounters an electrified orange ghost that has yellow sparks shooting out of its body. It's the 10,000 Volt Ghost, and it has the power to melt metal objects. Some say that an electrician crossed the wrong wires at the Winterhaven Power Plant and became this sparking spookster.

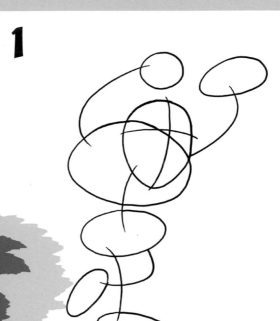

1

dRawing idea

When you color the 10,000 Volt Ghost, add lots of bright yellow sparks around the edges of its body.

Phantom

1

After the Mystery Inc. gang runs their boat aground on an island, they hike up to the creepy-looking Vasquez Castle to see if anyone can help them. It turns out that the castle is haunted by the Phantom. It's a creature covered in a long, flowing white robe, and it can walk through walls! But it's not all bad. Scooby and Shaggy are delighted to discover floating snacks inside the castle too!

2

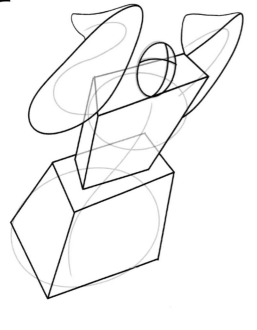

3

4

5

Black Knight

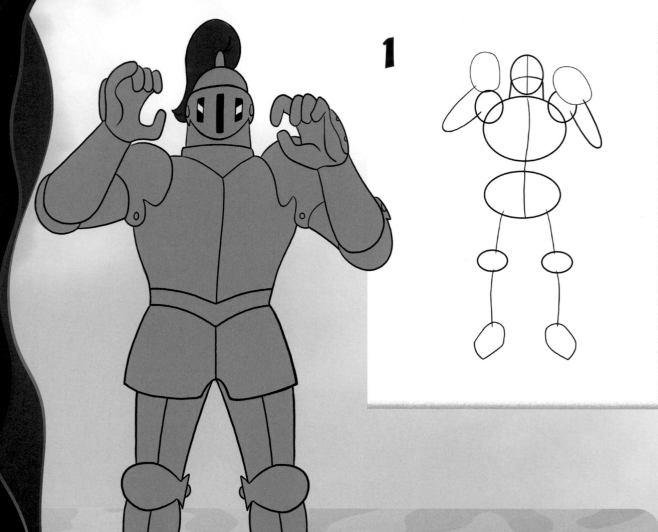

1

In their very first adventure together, Scooby-Doo and his pals investigate a haunted suit of armor in the Coolsonian Criminology Museum. Although at first it looks like an ordinary suit of black armor, the team is alarmed to discover that it's actually alive. Soon, the gang is on the run from the ominous Black Knight!

2

3

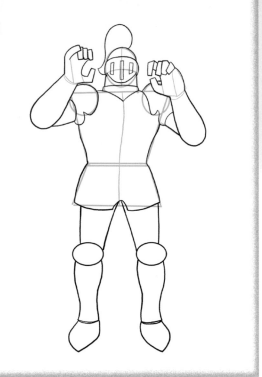

4

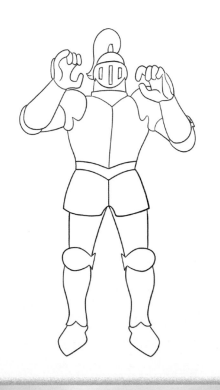

5

Ghost Clown

The Ghost Clown is haunting Barnstorm's Circus! Despite his silly-looking costume, this cackling clown is no joke. The Ghost Clown has an evil grin on his face, a menacing laugh, and glowing yellow eyes. He is also an expert hypnotist and uses a gold coin to hypnotize both Shaggy and Daphne! Will the hypnosis cure Shaggy of his endless appetite?

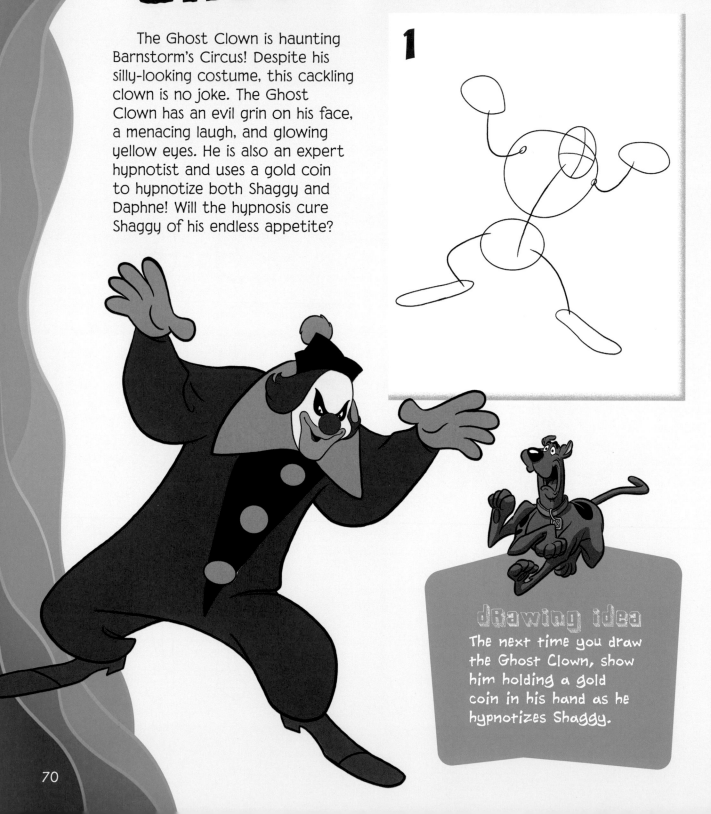

1

dRawing idea

The next time you draw the Ghost Clown, show him holding a gold coin in his hand as he hypnotizes Shaggy.

2

3

4

5

Redbeard's Ghost

1

"Ahhhhhr!" cries out the ghost of Redbeard. With his pirate hat, his flowing, red beard, and his razor-sharp sword, this sinister swashbuckler cuts a mean figure. But when he starts robbing freighter ships near Skull Island, Scooby and the gang know they must set sail to solve a mystery.

2

3

4

5

The Creeper

"Let's go, gang! We have a mystery to solve!" Fred calls out when trouble rears its head in town. It's the hulking hunchbacked creature known as the Creeper. This giant, green-faced brute has a violent temper. And after the monster robs a bank and disrupts a school dance, it's up to Mystery Inc. to trap this ghastly ghoul.

1

dRawing idea
Show Fred standing bravely in front of the giant Creeper.

2

3

4

5

Miner Forty Niner

1

When Scooby and the gang journey to a deserted mining town called Gold City, they meet up with a 150-year-old ghost miner. His name is the Miner Forty Niner, and he has scared off all of Gold City's residents and tourists. Will he scare off Mystery Inc., too, when they go digging for clues in his mine?

Ghost of Captain Cutler

1

Rocky Point Beach is the perfect spot for a beach party. But while gobbling down some tasty snacks—including chocolate-covered hot dogs for Scooby and Shaggy—the gang's fun comes to an end. A glowing, green scuba suit suddenly crashes the party! Local residents say that this spook is the ghost of the long-dead sailor, Captain Cutler.

2

3

4

5

Ghost of Mr. Hyde

1

"Jeepers!" yells Daphne when she discovers the Ghost of Mr. Hyde inside the Mystery Machine. This unwelcome intruder has pasty, green skin, long, bony fingers, and an evil, cackling laugh. Even more creepy, this ghastly ghost can also climb up the walls of buildings to escape the Mystery Inc. gang!

Escaping the Ghost Clown

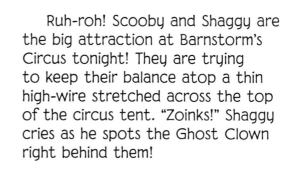

Ruh-roh! Scooby and Shaggy are the big attraction at Barnstorm's Circus tonight! They are trying to keep their balance atop a thin high-wire stretched across the top of the circus tent. "Zoinks!" Shaggy cries as he spots the Ghost Clown right behind them!

1

2

3

Charlie the Funland Robot

1

Look out! Here comes a menacing metal creature, known as Charlie the Funland Robot. Originally created to help run the Funland Amusement Park, someone has sabotaged the robot's circuits. Charlie is now programmed to destroy Mystery Inc.!

2

3

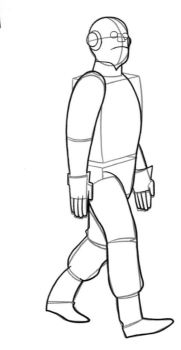

4

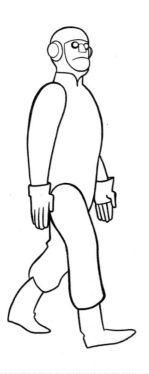

5

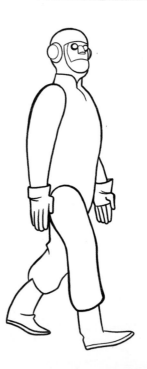

Snow Beast

A trip to the North Pole turns terrifying when the gang meets the Snow Beast. This giant robot looks like a furry dinosaur with razor-sharp claws and fangs. Weighing more than two tons, the Snow Beast towers over Scooby and the gang. Can they figure out a way to make this creature go extinct?

1

2

3

4

5

Spooky Space Kook

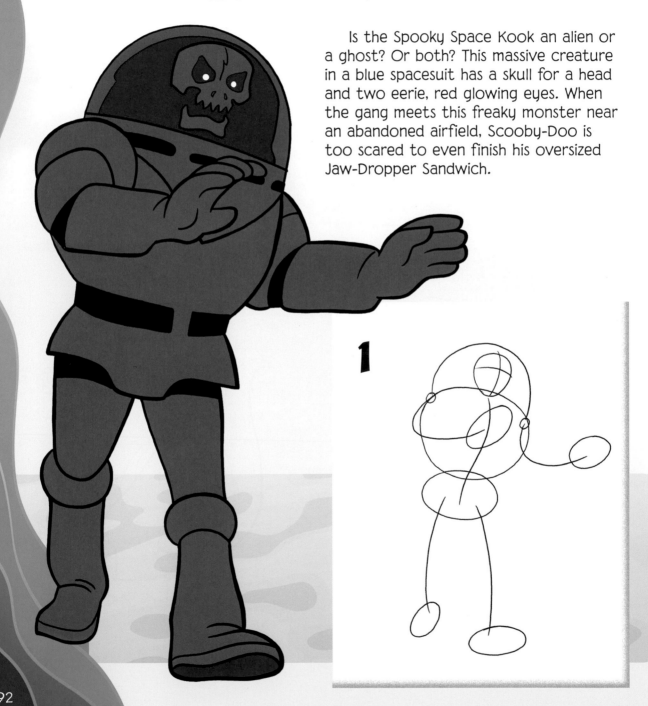

Is the Spooky Space Kook an alien or a ghost? Or both? This massive creature in a blue spacesuit has a skull for a head and two eerie, red glowing eyes. When the gang meets this freaky monster near an abandoned airfield, Scooby-Doo is too scared to even finish his oversized Jaw-Dropper Sandwich.

1

2

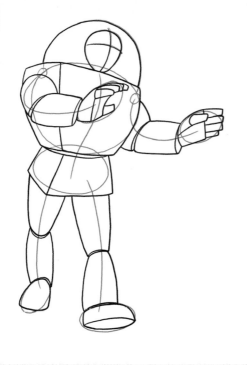

3

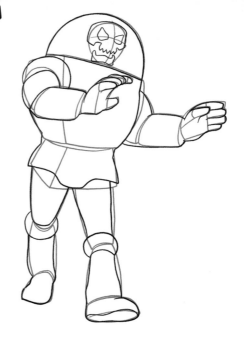

4

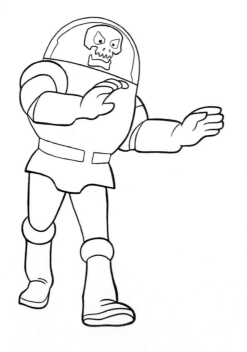

5

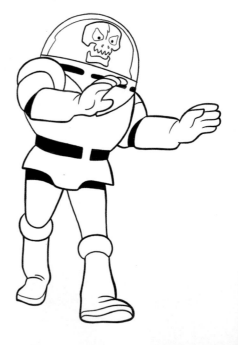

Future Monster

A time machine experiment goes horribly wrong when Professor Simon Grady accidentally brings a giant beast from 5,000 years in the future back to the present day. The Future Monster has huge bug-eyes and pointy claws and fangs. The creature is half-man and half-insect, and it is 100 percent creepy!

1

dRawing idea
Draw a time machine of your own design next to the Future Monster.

2

3

4

5

Evil Alien

Ruh-roh! Scooby-Doo, Shaggy, and Scrappy-Doo take a trip in a spaceship and meet this metal menace on another world. Even worse, the trio soon learns that this creature has the word "Evil" in its name. "Like, that's not a good sign," says Shaggy.

1

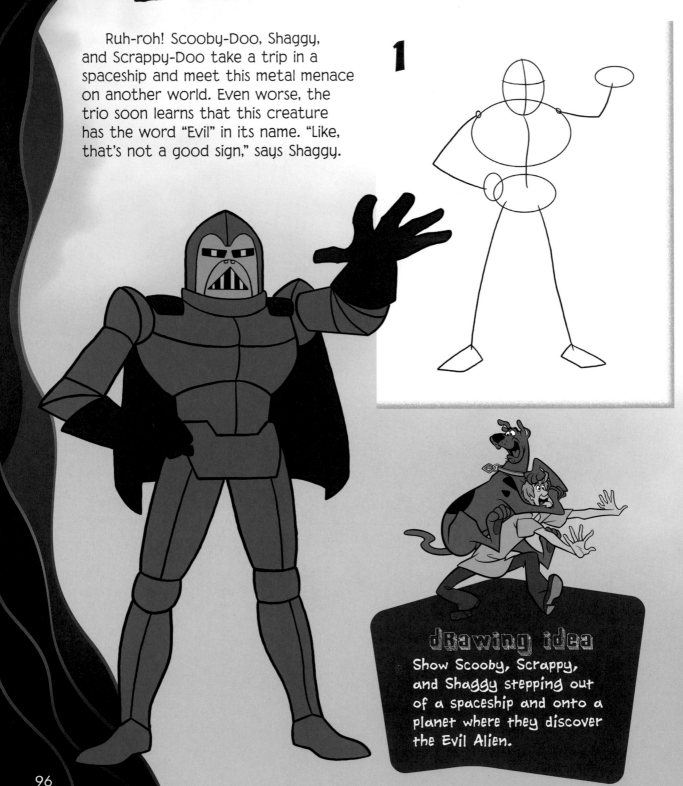

dRawing idea
Show Scooby, Scrappy, and Shaggy stepping out of a spaceship and onto a planet where they discover the Evil Alien.

2

3

4

5

Rawhide Red

1

A trip to a Wild West theme park called Robot Ranch gets a little too wild for Scooby and the gang. They meet up with the super-smart and super-dangerous Rawhide Red. Can the team figure out how to reprogram this risky robot?

2

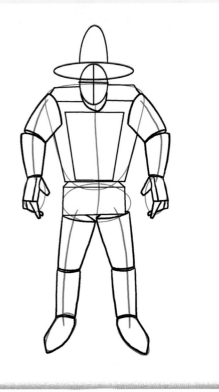

3

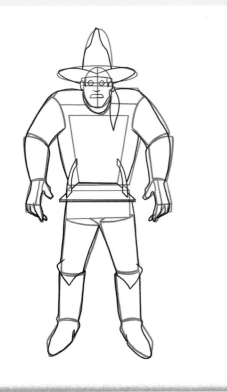

4

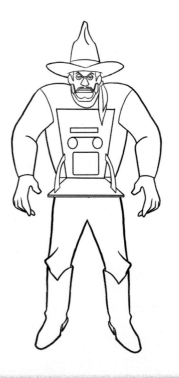

5

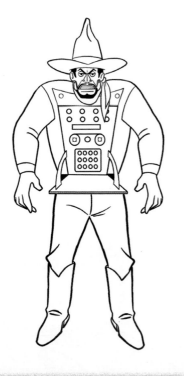

Mars Robot

BLAM! A rocket ship takes off for Mars with three accidental passengers—Scooby-Doo, Scrappy-Doo, and Shaggy! After landing on the Red Planet, the three encounter the Mars Robot. This metallic creature turns out to be a six-million-dollar research robot built on Earth!

1

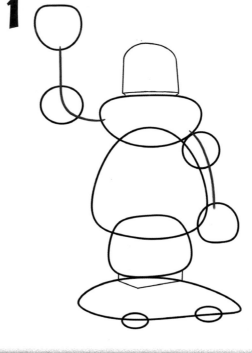

dRawing idea

Add a Martian background to your drawing. Then draw Scooby, Scrappy, and Shaggy too!

2

3

4

5

Monster Mouse

1

The massive Monster Mouse is ten times larger than the Mystery Inc. gang. It also has a bigger appetite than Shaggy and Scooby-Doo combined! Is this humongous rodent a scientific experiment gone wrong or an evildoer's mechanical robot? It's up to Scooby and the gang to figure it out.

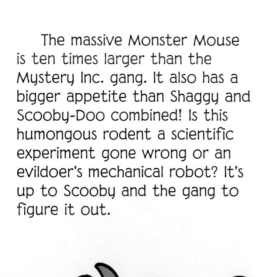

dRawing idea

The next time you draw Monster Mouse, show it grabbing Scooby-Doo with one of its giant paws.

2

3

4

5

Nuclear Alien

When a billion dollars goes missing from a nuclear research laboratory, all clues point to a glowing, radioactive space alien as the robber! "It looks like we have a mystery to solve," declares Fred, as the team tracks down the creepy-looking creature.

1

dRawing idea

Show Daphne bravely confronting the Nuclear Alien. Be sure to draw a glow around the creature.

2

3

4

5

Body-Snatcher Alien

1

"Ruh-roh!" Scooby cries when he first sees the Body-Snatcher Alien. This creepy creature has green skin, a cone-shaped head, and many legs. It has traveled to Earth with a triple-trouble plan to create clones of Scooby, Scrappy, and Shaggy!

drawing idea

Show Scooby, Scrappy, and Shaggy running away from the evil Body-Snatcher Alien.

2

3

4

5

Escaping Charlie the Funland Robot

"Like, get us out of here!" yells Shaggy as a fun day at the amusement park turns frightfully freaky! He and Scooby are on the run from a rampaging robot. Will they get chased down by Charlie or escape the mechanical menace?

1

2

3

4

5

Published by Capstone Press, an imprint of Capstone.
1710 Roe Crest Drive
North Mankato, Minnesota 56003
capstonepub.com

Library of Congress Cataloging-in-Publication Data
is available on the Library of Congress website.

ISBN: 9781666382440 (paperback)
ISBN: 9781666390391 (eBook PDF)

Summary: Solve the mystery behind drawing Scooby-Doo and the show's most popular
monsters, robots, aliens, and more! With step-by-step instructions, you'll learn to sketch
more than 35 classic characters and two awesome versions of the Mystery Machine. Drawing
Scooby-Doo has never been more fun and easy!

Editorial Credits
Christopher Harbo, Editor; Tracy Davies, Designer;
Katy LaVigne, Pre-Media Specialist

Design Elements
Shutterstock: BNP Design Studio, Ori Artiste, sidmay

The publisher and the author shall not be liable for any damages allegedly arising
from the information in this book, and they specifically disclaim any liability from the
use or application of any of the contents of this book.